100+ Essential Act... Sight Words

Table of Contents

Sight Words

Directions: Trace the sight word.

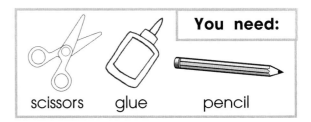

You need:

scissors   glue   pencil

Practice writing the sight word.

_____

Cut and paste the sight word.

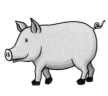
pig

cat

cow

puppy

Name _____

Sight Words

Directions: Trace the sight word.

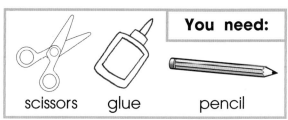

Practice writing the sight word.

Cut and paste the sight word.

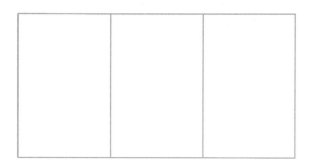

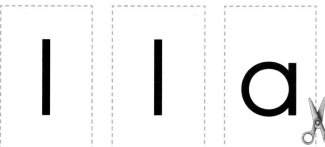

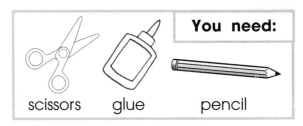
Sight Words

Directions: Trace the sight word.

You need:

scissors   glue   pencil

Practice writing the sight word.

Cut and paste the sight word.

Name _____

Sight Words

Directions: Trace the sight word.

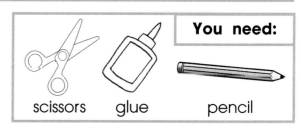

Practice writing the sight word.

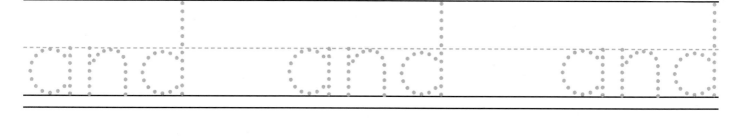

Cut and paste the sight word.

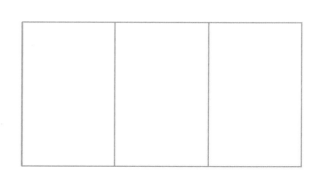

100+ Essential Activities for Sight Words • ©2011 Newmark Learning, LLC

Name _____

Sight Words

Directions: Trace the sight word.

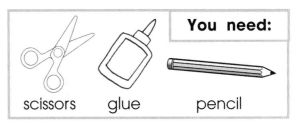

Practice writing the sight word.

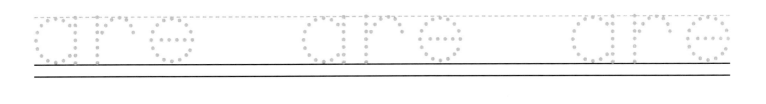

Cut and paste the sight word.

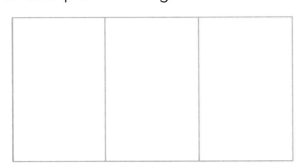 

 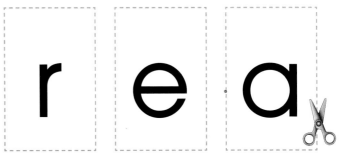

Name _____

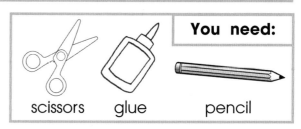

You need:

scissors   glue   pencil

Sight Words

Directions: Trace the sight word.

Practice writing the sight word.

Cut and paste the sight word.

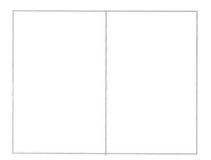

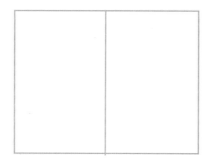

t a   t a   t a

100+ Essential Activities for Sight Words • ©2011 Newmark Learning, LLC

Sight Words

Directions: Trace the sight word.

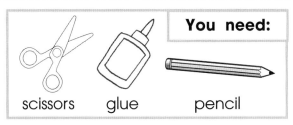

You need:
scissors   glue   pencil

be

be

Practice writing the sight word.

Cut and paste the sight word.

e   b   e   b   e   b

Name _____

Sight Words

Directions: Trace the sight word.

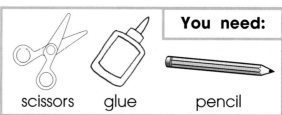

You need:

scissors   glue   pencil

big   big

Practice writing the sight word.

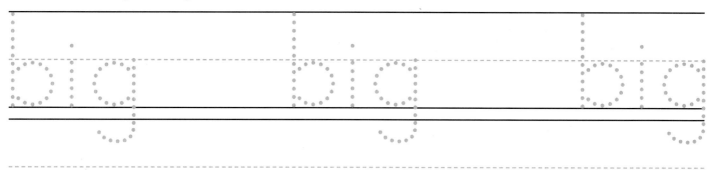

Cut and paste the sight word.

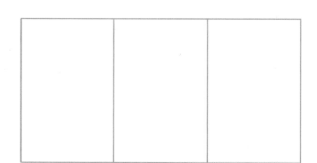

g   i   b

i   g   b

100+ Essential Activities for Sight Words • ©2011 Newmark Learning, LLC

Sight Words

Directions: Trace the sight word.

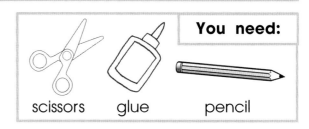

Practice writing the sight word.

_____

can   can   can

Cut and paste the sight word.

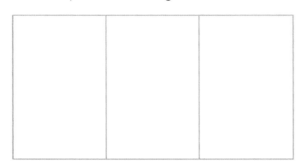

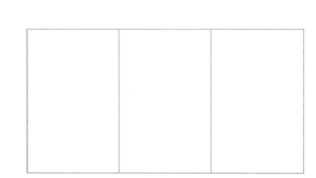

n   a   c   a   n   c

Name _____

Sight Words

Directions: Trace the sight word.

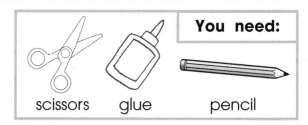

You need:
scissors   glue   pencil

dad

Practice writing the sight word.

Cut and paste the sight word.

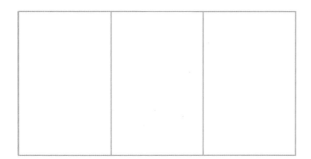

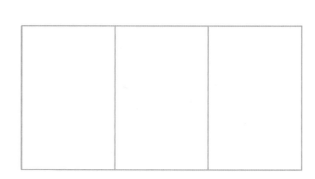

Sight Words

Directions: Trace the sight word.

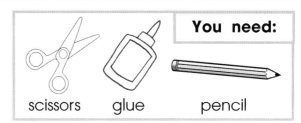

You need:

scissors   glue   pencil

Practice writing the sight word.

Cut and paste the sight word.

Name _____

Sight Words

Directions: Trace the sight word.

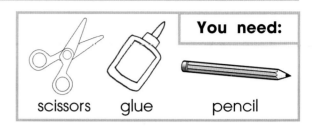

You need:

scissors   glue   pencil

Practice writing the sight word.

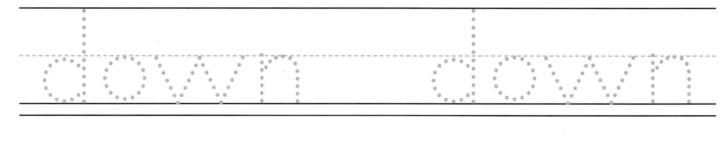

Cut and paste the sight word.

100+ Essential Activities for Sight Words • ©2011 Newmark Learning, LLC

Name _____

Sight Words

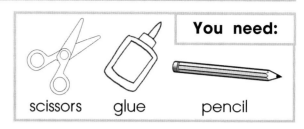

Directions: Trace the sight word.

Practice writing the sight word.

Cut and paste the sight word.

Name _____

Sight Words

Directions: Trace the sight word.

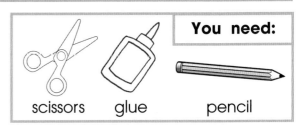
You need:
scissors   glue   pencil

Practice writing the sight word.

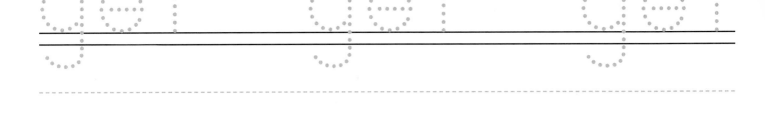

Cut and paste the sight word.

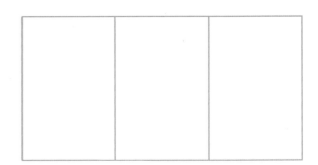

Name _____

Sight Words

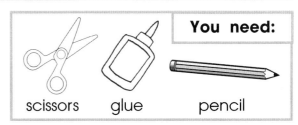

Directions: Trace the sight word.

go   go

Practice writing the sight word.

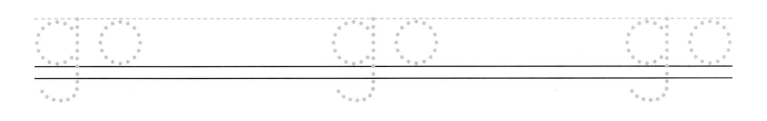

Cut and paste the sight word.

o g   o g   o g

Name _____

Sight Words

Directions: Trace the sight word.

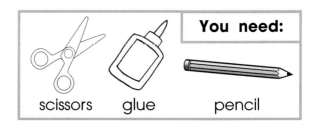

You need:

scissors   glue   pencil

goes

Practice writing the sight word.

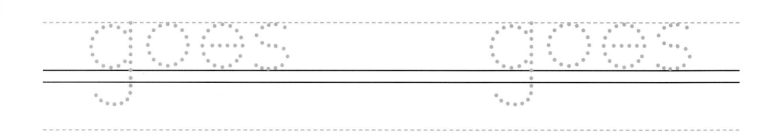

Cut and paste the sight word.

s   e   o   g

Sight Words

Directions: Trace the sight word.

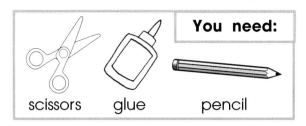

Practice writing the sight word.

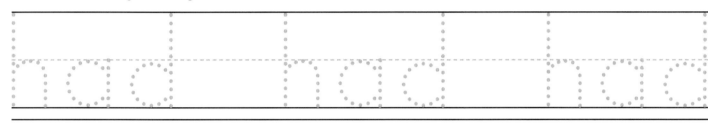

Cut and paste the sight word.

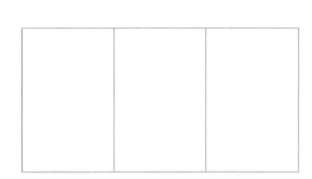

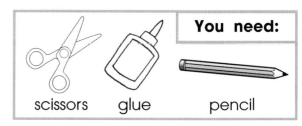
Name _____

Sight Words

Directions: Trace the sight word.

has   has

Practice writing the sight word.

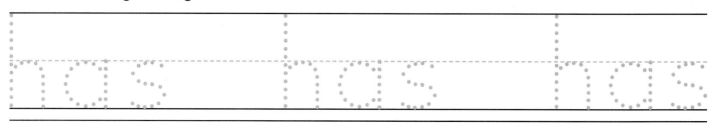

Cut and paste the sight word.

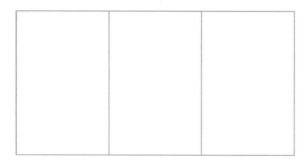

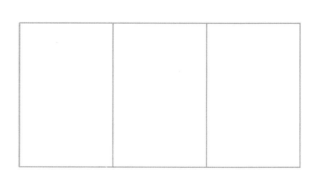

Sight Words

Directions: Trace the sight word.

You need:

scissors   glue   pencil

Practice writing the sight word.

Cut and paste the sight word.

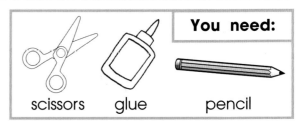
Name _____

Sight Words

Directions: Trace the sight word.

You need:

scissors   glue   pencil

Practice writing the sight word.

Cut and paste the sight word.

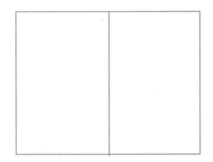

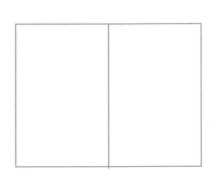

100+ Essential Activities for Sight Words • ©2011 Newmark Learning, LLC

Sight Words

Directions: Trace the sight word.

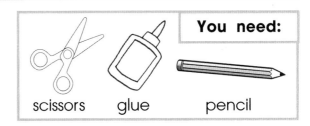

You need:

scissors   glue   pencil

Practice writing the sight word.

Cut and paste the sight word.

Name _____

Sight Words

Directions: Trace the sight word.

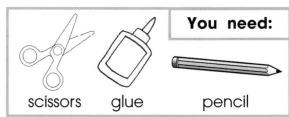

You need:

scissors   glue   pencil

 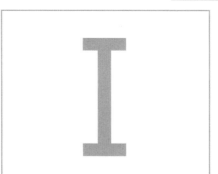 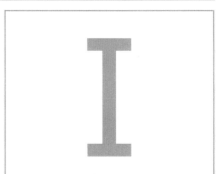

Practice writing the sight word.

_____

Cut and paste the sight word.

run .

 kick .

jump .

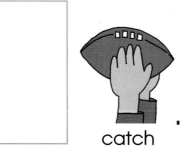 catch .

Name _____

Sight Words

Directions: Trace the sight word.

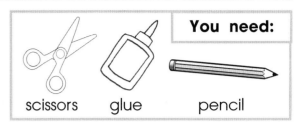

You need:

scissors   glue   pencil

Practice writing the sight word.

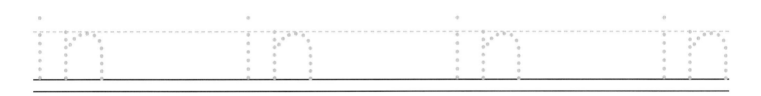

Cut and paste the sight word.

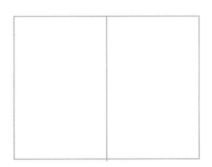

Name _____

Sight Words

Directions: Trace the sight word.

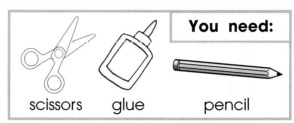
You need:
scissors   glue   pencil

is   is

Practice writing the sight word.

is   is   is   is

Cut and paste the sight word.

s i s i s i

100+ Essential Activities for Sight Words • ©2011 Newmark Learning, LLC

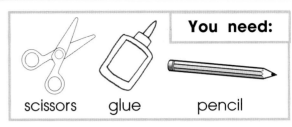
Sight Words

Directions: Trace the sight word.

You need:

scissors   glue   pencil

Practice writing the sight word.

Cut and paste the sight word.

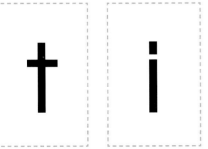

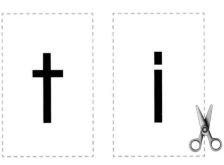

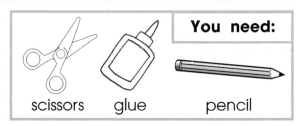

Name _____

Sight Words

Directions: Trace the sight word.

Practice writing the sight word.

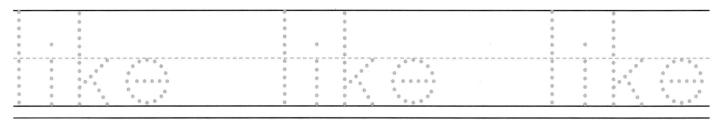

Cut and paste the sight word.

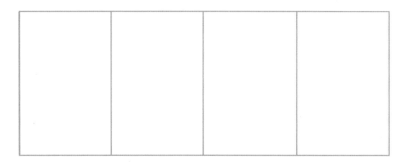

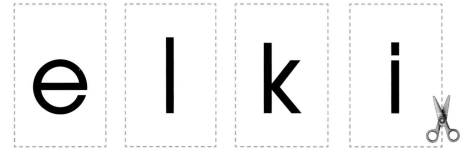

28

100+ Essential Activities for Sight Words • ©2011 Newmark Learning, LLC

Name _____

Sight Words

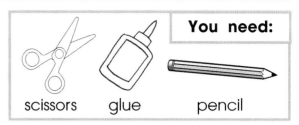

You need:

scissors   glue   pencil

Directions: Trace the sight word.

Practice writing the sight word.

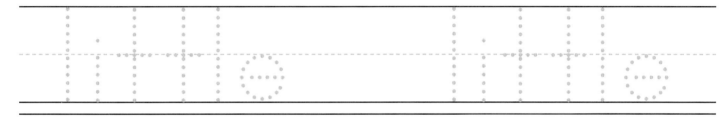

Cut and paste the sight word.

t   e   l   t   i   l

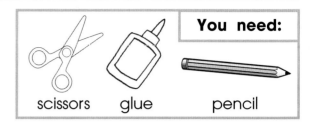
Name _____

Sight Words

Directions: Trace the sight word.

You need:

scissors   glue   pencil

Practice writing the sight word.

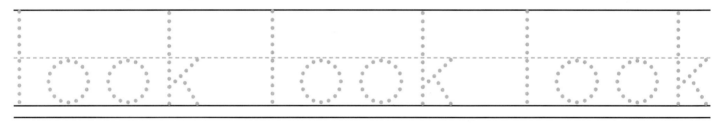

Cut and paste the sight word.

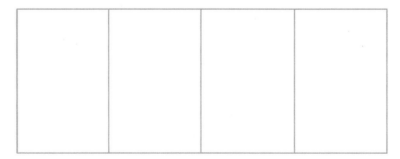

30

Name _____

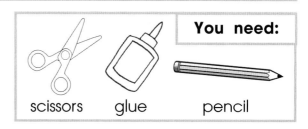

You need:

scissors   glue   pencil

Sight Words

Directions: Trace the sight word.

Practice writing the sight word.

_____

me   me   me

- -

_____

Cut and paste the sight word.

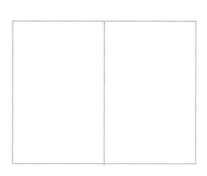

e   m   m   e   e   m

Sight Words

Directions: Trace the sight word.

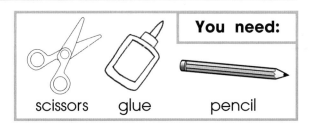

You need:

scissors   glue   pencil

Practice writing the sight word.

Cut and paste the sight word.

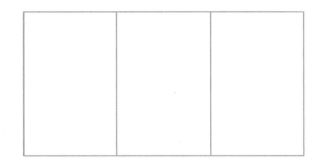

Sight Words

SIGHT WORD READERS

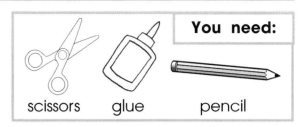

You need:
scissors glue pencil

Directions: Trace the sight word.

Practice writing the sight word.

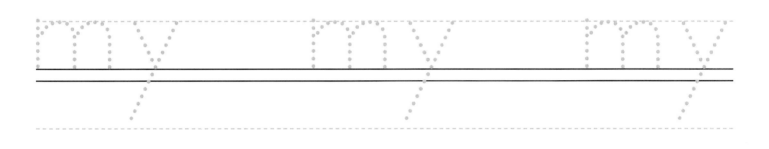

Cut and paste the sight word.

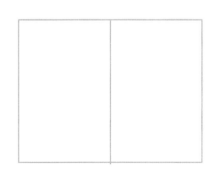

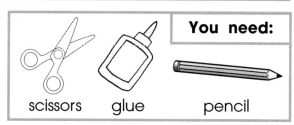
Sight Words

Directions: Trace the sight word.

You need:

scissors glue pencil

Practice writing the sight word.

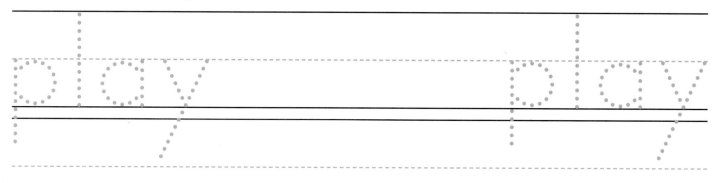

Cut and paste the sight word.

100+ Essential Activities for Sight Words • ©2011 Newmark Learning, LLC

Name _____

Sight Words

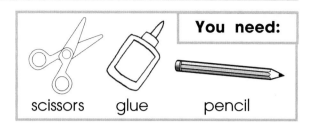

Directions: Trace the sight word.

said

Practice writing the sight word.

said   said

Cut and paste the sight word.

i d a s

Name _____

Sight Words

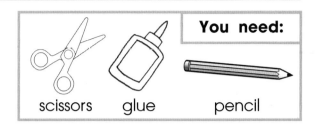
Directions: Trace the sight word.

see

Practice writing the sight word.

see   see   see

Cut and paste the sight word.

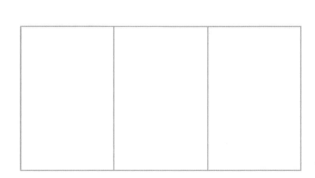

e   s   e   e   e   s

Name _____

Sight Words

Directions: Trace the sight word.

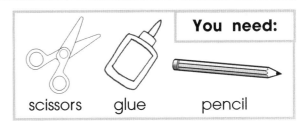
she

Practice writing the sight word.

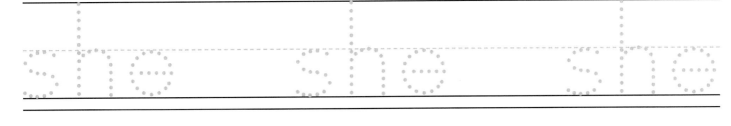

Cut and paste the sight word.

e   s   h   h   e   s

Sight Words

Directions: Trace the sight word.

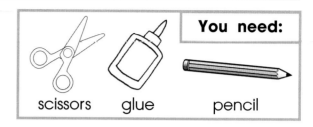

You need:

scissors   glue   pencil

Practice writing the sight word.

Cut and paste the sight word.

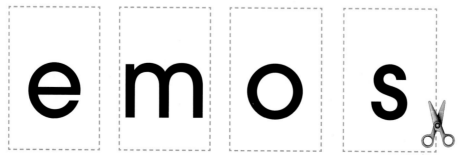

Sight Words

Directions: Trace the sight word.

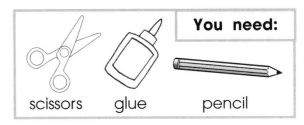

Practice writing the sight word.

Cut and paste the sight word.

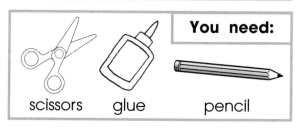
Name _____

Sight Words

Directions: Trace the sight word.

You need:

scissors   glue   pencil

Practice writing the sight word.

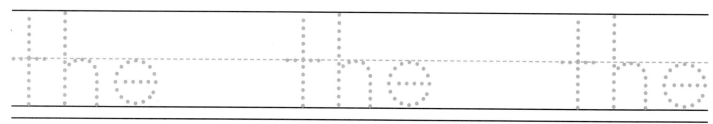

Cut and paste the sight word.

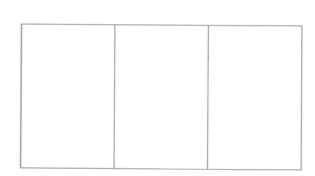

Sight Words

Directions: Trace the sight word.

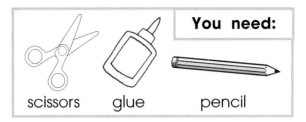

You need:

scissors   glue   pencil

Practice writing the sight word.

there   there

Cut and paste the sight word.

e h t e r

Sight Words

Directions: Trace the sight word.

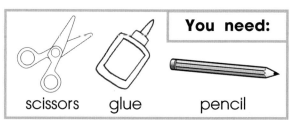

Practice writing the sight word.

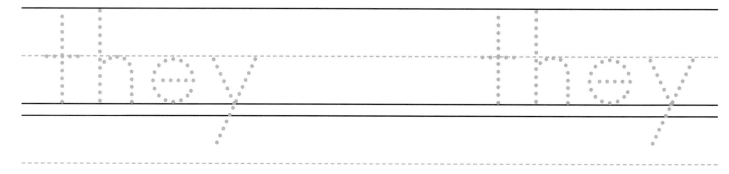

Cut and paste the sight word.

100+ Essential Activities for Sight Words • ©2011 Newmark Learning, LLC

Sight Words

Directions: Trace the sight word.

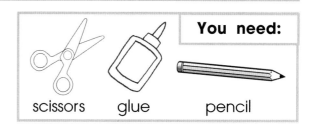

scissors   glue   pencil

You need:

Practice writing the sight word.

Cut and paste the sight word.

i   t   s   h

Name _____

Sight Words

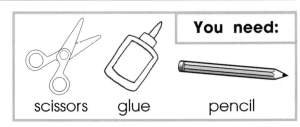

You need:

scissors   glue   pencil

Directions: Trace the sight word.

Practice writing the sight word.

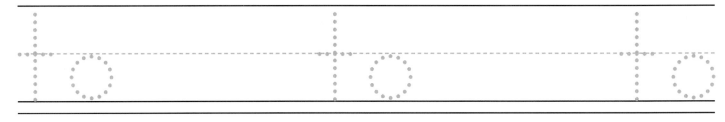

Cut and paste the sight word.

 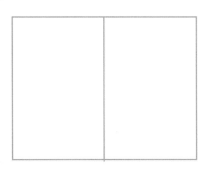 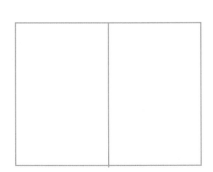

  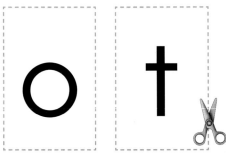

Sight Words

Directions: Trace the sight word.

You need:

scissors   glue   pencil

Practice writing the sight word.

_____

Cut and paste the sight word.

Name _____

Sight Words

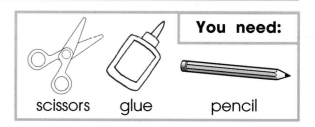

You need:

scissors   glue   pencil

Directions: Trace the sight word.

Practice writing the sight word.

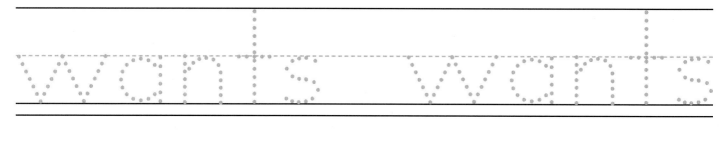

Cut and paste the sight word.

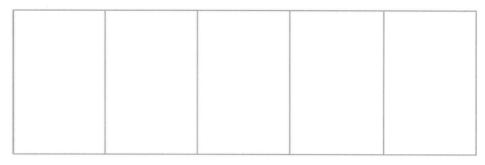

n   s   t   w   a

Name _____

Sight Words

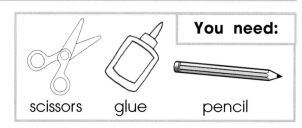

You need:

scissors   glue   pencil

Directions: Trace the sight word.

Practice writing the sight word.

_____

_____

_ _

_____

Cut and paste the sight word.

Name _____

Sight Words

Directions: Trace the sight word.

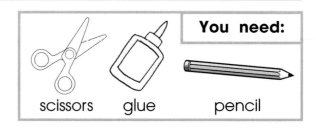

You need:

scissors   glue   pencil

went

Practice writing the sight word.

went   went

Cut and paste the sight word.

e   t   w   n

100+ Essential Activities for Sight Words • ©2011 Newmark Learning, LLC

Sight Words

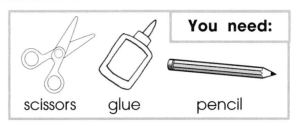

You need:

scissors   glue   pencil

Directions: Trace the sight word.

Practice writing the sight word.

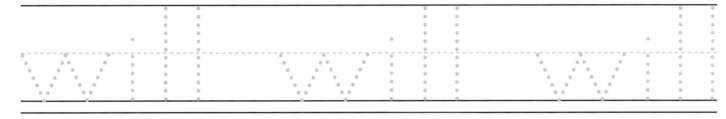

Cut and paste the sight word.

l   i   w   l

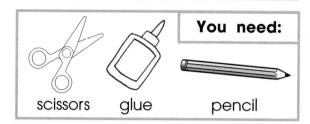

Name _____

Sight Words

Directions: Trace the sight word.

You need:

scissors   glue   pencil

Practice writing the sight word.

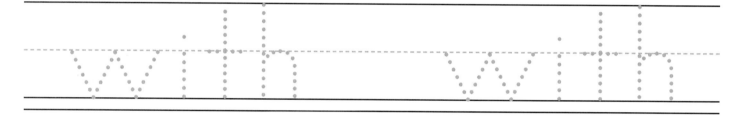

Cut and paste the sight word.

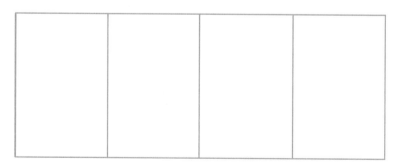

h   i   w   t

50

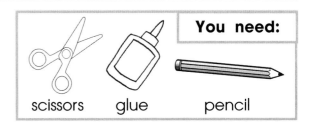

Sight Words

Directions: Trace the sight word.

Practice writing the sight word.

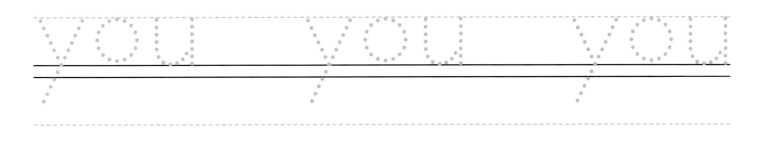

Cut and paste the sight word.

Name _____

Sight Word Sort

Directions:
Cut and paste each sight word into the correct column.

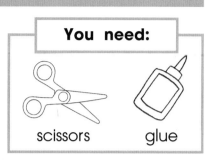

You need:

scissors   glue

1 Letter

2 Letters

3 Letters

a	are	can	he
I	it	me	my
she	the	we	you

100+ Essential Activities for Sight Words • ©2011 Newmark Learning, LLC

Name _____

Sight Word Sort

You need:

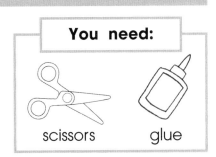

scissors   glue

Directions:
Cut and paste each sight word into the correct column.

2 Letters

3 Letters

4 Letters

at	dad	do	eat
has	in	is	like
see	she	to	went

Name _____

Sight Word Sort

Directions:
Cut and paste each sight word into the correct column.

You need:

scissors   glue

2 Letters

3 Letters

4 Letters

am	are	be	can
go	has	here	in
look	see	up	will

100+ Essential Activities for Sight Words • ©2011 Newmark Learning, LLC

Name _____

Sight Word Sort

Directions:
Cut and paste each sight word into the correct column.

3 Letters

4 Letters

5 Letters

all	dad	get	goes
mom	play	some	that
there	wants	with	you

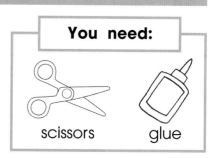

Sight Word Readers

Name _____

Sight Word Sort

Directions:
Cut and paste each sight word into the correct column.

You need:

scissors   glue

3 Letters

4 Letters

5 Letters

6 Letters

and	big	down	eat
had	have	little	mom
said	they	this	wants

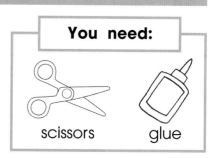

100+ Essential Activities for Sight Words • ©2011 Newmark Learning, LLC

Sight Word Search

You need:

pencil

Directions:
Read the list of sight words.
Then circle each word in the puzzle.

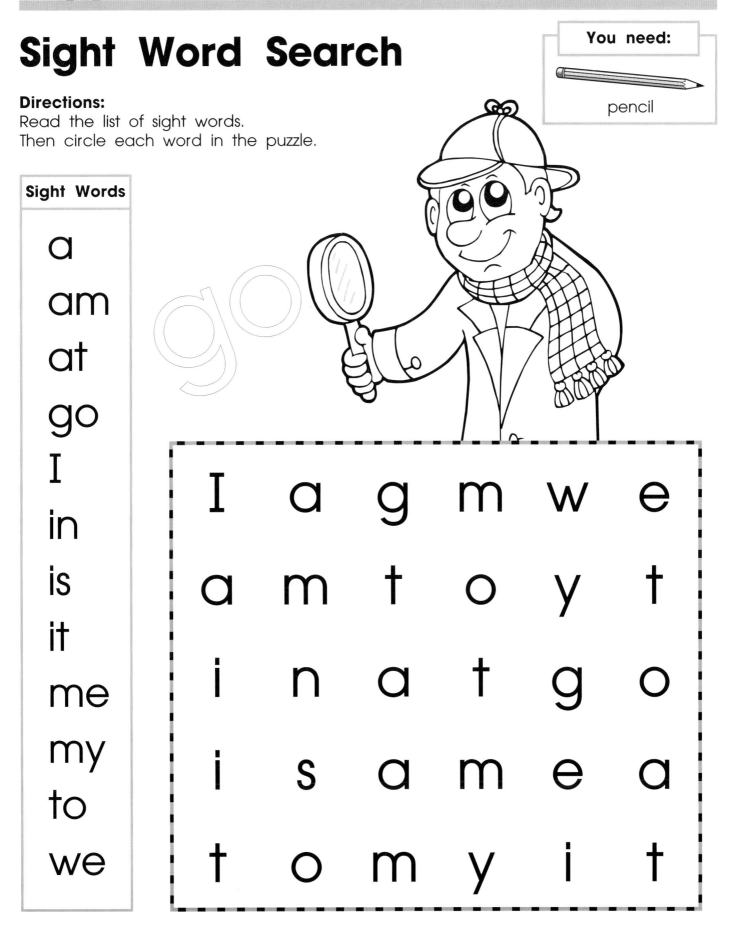

Sight Words

a
am
at
go
I
in
is
it
me
my
to
we

I a g m w e
a m t o y t
i n a t g o
i s a m e a
t o m y i t

Sight Word Search

Directions:
Read the list of sight words.
Then circle each word in the puzzle.

big

Sight Words

are

big

have

he

here

like

little

look

a	r	e	b	i	g
r	r	h	a	v	e
e	h	e	r	e	l
l	i	k	e	g	i
h	e	l	o	o	k
l	i	t	t	l	e

Name _____

Sight Word Search

Directions:
Read the list of sight words.
Then circle each word in the puzzle.

Sight Words

can
has
play
see
she
the
this
you

h	a	s	s	e	e
s	h	e	y	o	u
t	h	e	c	a	n
p	l	a	y	a	m
t	h	i	s	t	n

Name _____

Sight Word Search

You need:

pencil

Directions:
Read the list of sight words.
Then circle each word in the puzzle.

Sight Words
and
dad
down
get
they
went
with

w	e	n	t	d	o
i	t	g	e	o	d
t	h	e	y	w	a
h	e	t	a	n	d
i	d	o	w	n	a
t	h	e	y	e	d

Name _____

Sight Word Search

Directions:
Read the list of sight words.
Then circle each word in the puzzle.

Sight Words
had
said
some
there
up
wants
will

w	a	n	t	s	o
i	u	p	h	a	d
l	p	s	a	i	d
l	g	h	a	d	u
s	o	m	e	u	p
t	h	e	r	e	p

Name _____

Sight Word Search

You need:

pencil

Directions:
Read the list of sight words.
Then circle each word in the puzzle.

do

Sight Words
all
be
do
eat
goes
mom
that

m	o	m	a	l	l
o	e	a	t	p	d
m	a	b	e	d	o
c	t	g	o	e	s
t	h	a	t	b	e

Name _____

Animals on the Farm

You need:

pencil

Directions:
Find the sight words on the farm.

Word Bank

see   some   we

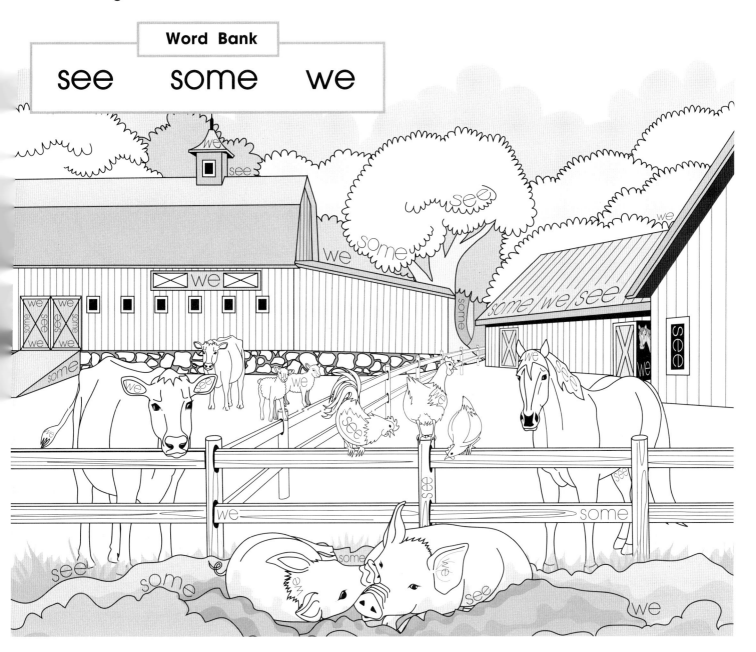

Directions: Practice writing the sight words.

We see some

Name _____

At the Shore

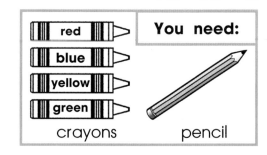

You need:

red
blue
yellow
green

crayons   pencil

Directions:

Color each sight word according to the key below.

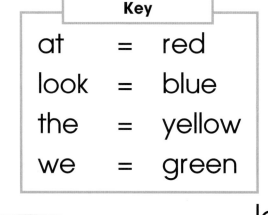

Key		
at	=	red
look	=	blue
the	=	yellow
we	=	green

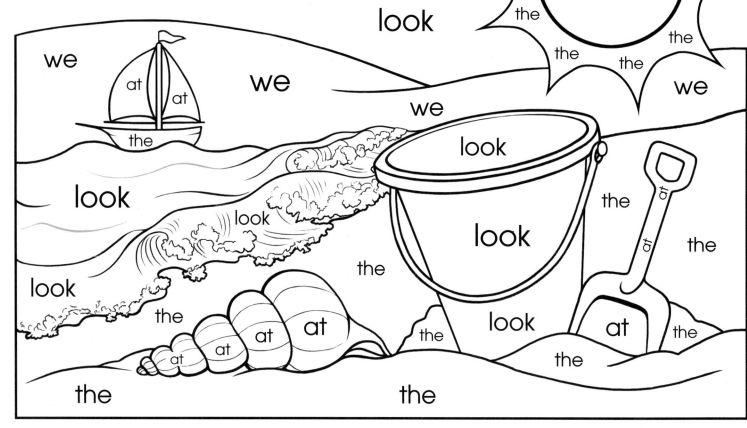

Directions: Practice writing the sight words.

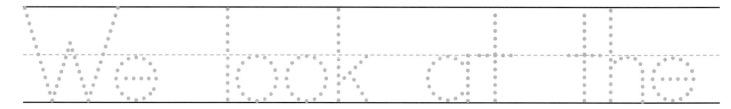

    100+ Essential Activities for Sight Words • ©2011 Newmark Learning, LLC

Going Up and Down

Directions:
Trace the sight words. Then cut and paste the pictures to complete each sentence.

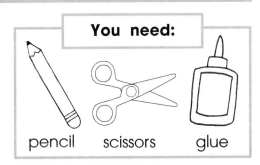
They go _____ up the

steps .

They go _____

slide .

They go _____ the

ramp .

They _____ go down the

rope .

ramp

rope

slide

steps

I Am Active

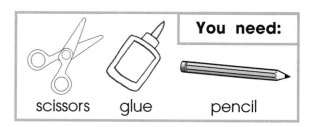

You need:

scissors   glue   pencil

Directions:

Cut and paste the pictures to complete each sentence. Then make your own sentence. Practice writing the sight words.

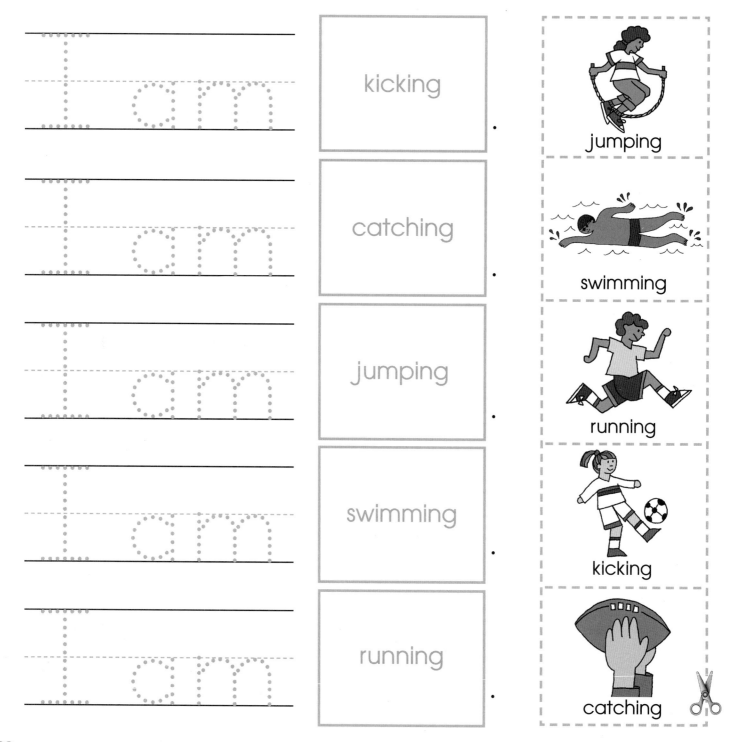

I am _____

I am _____

I am _____

I am _____

I am _____

kicking

catching

jumping

swimming

running

jumping

swimming

running

kicking

catching

Name _____

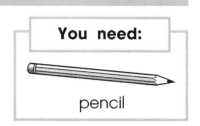
You need:

pencil

I Go!

Directions:
Underline each sight word you see.

Word Bank
a   go   I   in

I	r	m	g	o
i	n	x	a	z

b	I	p
g	o	f
i	n	t	a

x	p	I	g	o
r	y	i	n	a

c	I	g	o	w
i	n	z	r	a

Name _____

I Like the Spring!

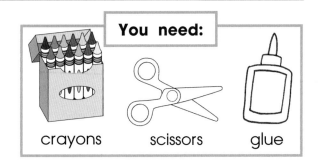

You need:

crayons   scissors   glue

Directions:

Cut out the pictures that show spring. Paste the pictures to complete the puzzle. Then color the picture!

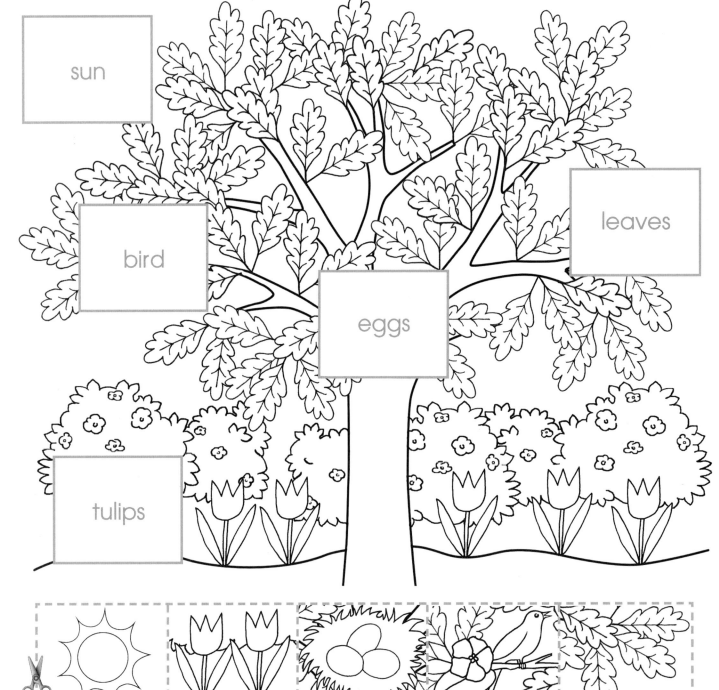

sun

bird

leaves

eggs

tulips

sun   tulips   eggs   bird   leaves

Name _____

In the Water

Directions:
Find the sight words at the water park. Then color the picture.

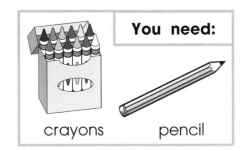

You need:

crayons   pencil

Word Bank

I   in   play   the

Directions: Practice writing the sight words.

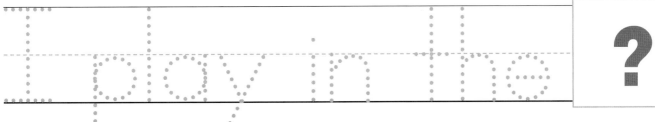

I play in the [?]

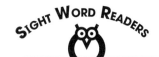

Name ______________________________

Look and See

You need:

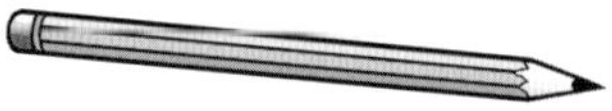

pencil

Directions:
Circle each sight word you see.

Word Bank

at look that

m	y	l	o	o	k
a	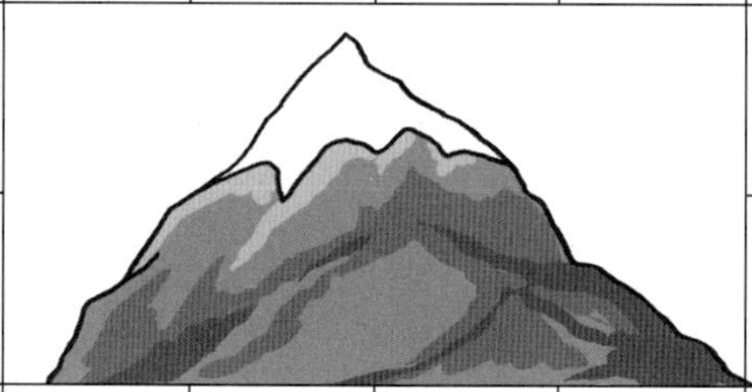				o
t					a
z	o	t	h	a	t

l	o	o	k	a	t
o	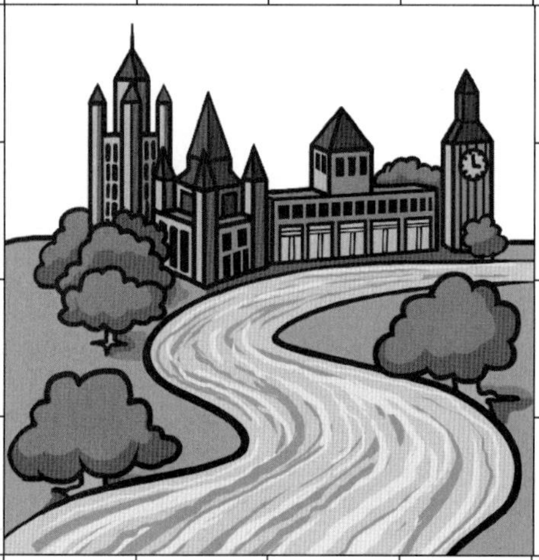				h
o					a
k					t
z					a
a	x	t	h	a	t

w	l	o	o	k
l	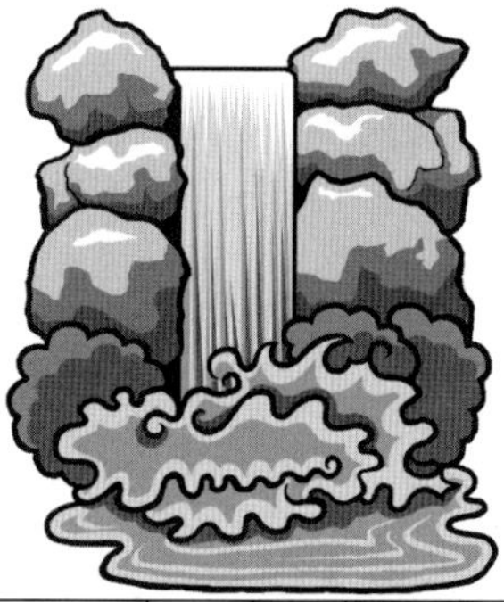			t
o				h
o				a
k	a	n	a	t

t	h	a	t	l
y	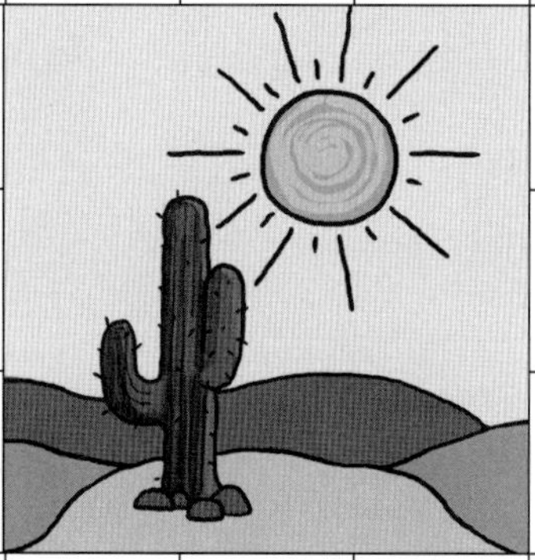			o
p				o
e				k
a	t	h	a	t

a	t	h	a	t	t
t	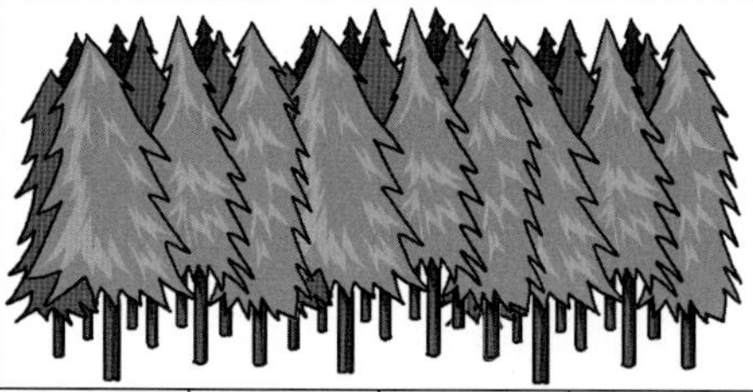				h
m					a
l	o	o	k	a	t

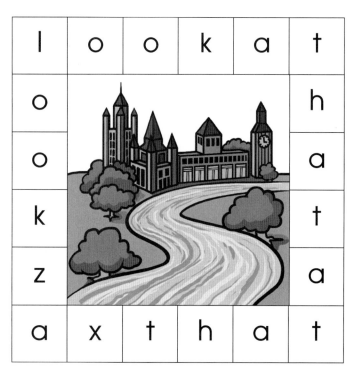

Name _____

Look at the Sky

You need:

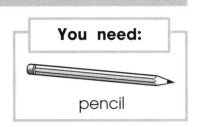

pencil

Directions:
Connect each sight word. Make a path for the spaceship.

Word Bank

| can | see | the | you |

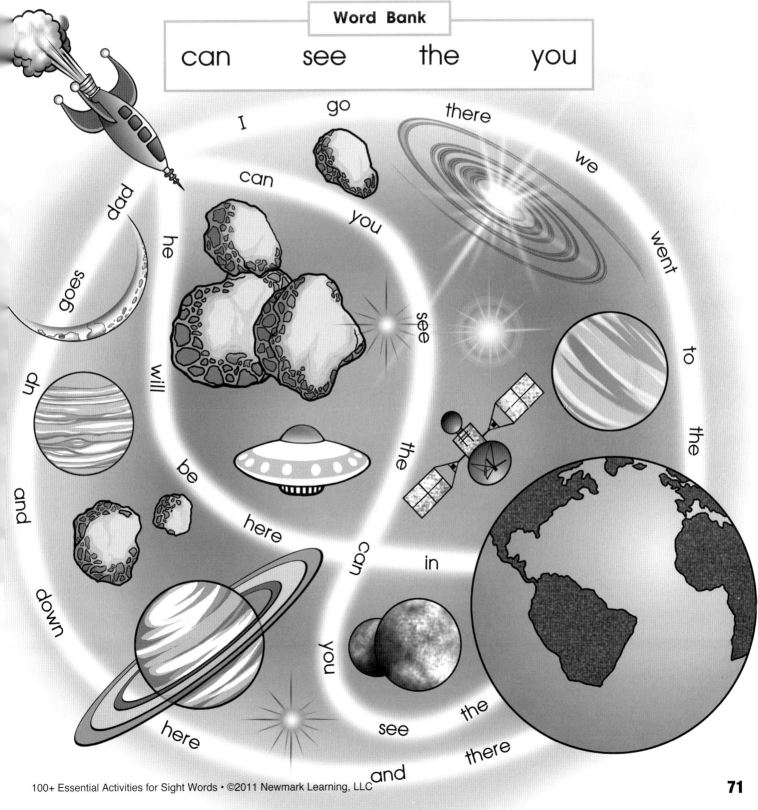

Look at the Weather

Directions:
Cut and paste each word to complete the sentence.

You need:
scissors   glue

Monday: [I] can [see] the .
sun

Tuesday: I [can] see [the] .
lightning

Wednesday: I can [see] the .
snow

Thursday: I can see [the] .
rain

Friday: [I] [can] see the .
wind

| I | can | see | the |
| I | can | see | the |

100+ Essential Activities for Sight Words • ©2011 Newmark Learning, LLC

Name _____

See the Birds

Directions: Find the sight words at the bird sanctuary.
Then color the picture.

You need:

crayons   pencil

Word Bank

| do | see | the | you |

Directions: Practice writing the sight words.

Do you see the

Name _____

Snack Time

You need:

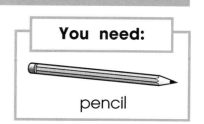

pencil

Directions:
Look at the picture. Then check off each true statement.

☐ They had some [celery]. celery

☐ They had some [cheese]. cheese

☐ They had some [crackers]. crackers

☐ They had some [carrots]. carrots

☐ They had some [pretzels]. pretzels

☐ They had some [cucumbers]. cucumbers

Directions: Practice writing the sight words.

They had some

Name _____

They Grow Plants

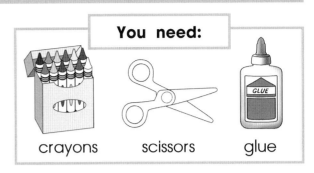

Directions:

Cut out the pictures. Paste the pictures to complete the puzzle. Then color the picture!

corn

pumpkins   tomatoes   peppers   watermelon

corn   peppers   pumpkins   tomatoes   watermelon

We Have Fruit

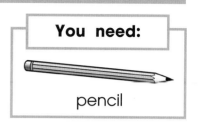
Directions:
Look at the picture. Then check off each true statement.

fruit

☐ We have  .
apples

☐ We have 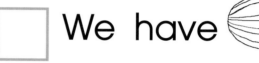 .
watermelon

☐ We have  .
pears

☐ We have  .
strawberries

☐ We have 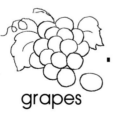 .
grapes

☐ We have 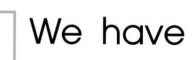 .
cherries

Directions: Practice writing the sight words.

We have

We Like Vegetables

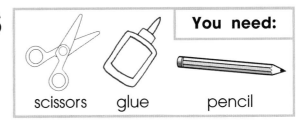
Directions:
Trace the sight words. Then cut and paste the pictures to complete each sentence.

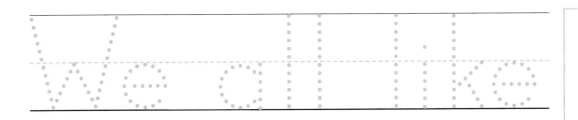

peppers .

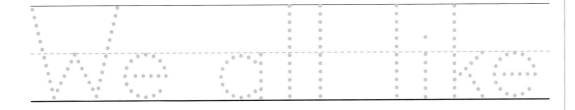

cucumbers .

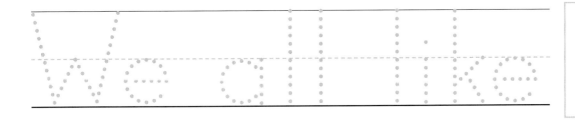

carrots .

beans .

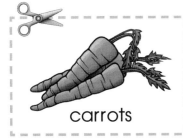

carrots

cucumbers

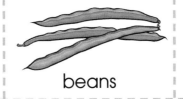

beans

peppers

What Goes Up?

Directions:
Cut and paste the pictures to complete each sentence.

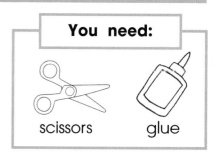
That | kite | goes up.

That | balloon | goes up.

That | rocket | goes up.

That | plane | goes up.

That | ball | goes up.

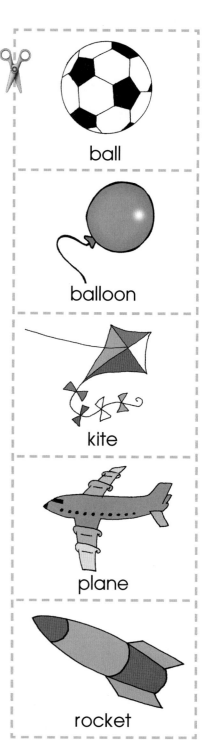

ball

balloon

kite

plane

rocket

Name _____

Animal Babies

Directions:
Cut and paste the pictures to complete each sentence. Practice writing the sight words.

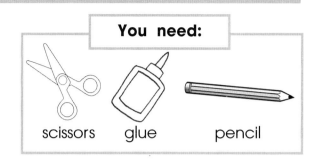
____ play with 1

I ____ with 2

____ play with 3

I ____ with 4

____ play with 5

| chick |
| puppies |
| lambs |
| bunnies |
| kittens |

bunnies

lambs

chick

kittens

puppies

Name _____

Big Pet, Little Pet

Directions:
Color each pet. Then cut and paste in the word that describes the pet.

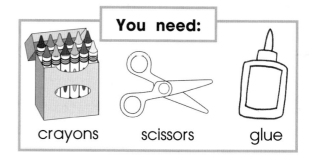

You need:

crayons   scissors   glue

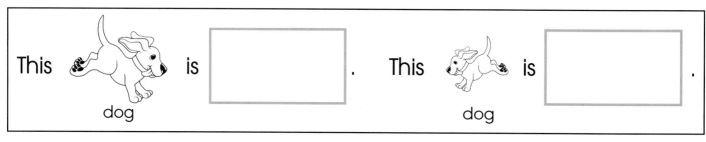

This [dog] is [____]. This [dog] is [____].

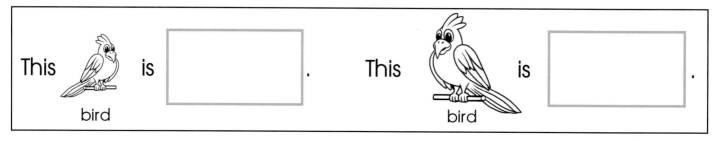

This [bird] is [____]. This [bird] is [____].

This [fish] is [____]. This [fish] is [____].

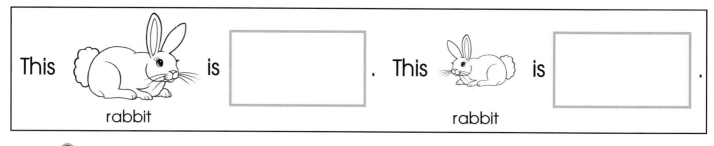

This [rabbit] is [____]. This [rabbit] is [____].

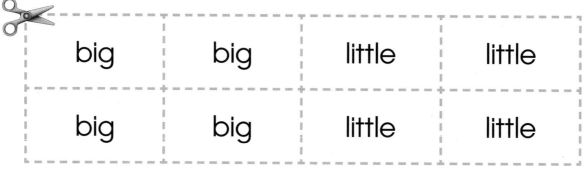

| big | big | little | little |
| big | big | little | little |

Count Around the Room

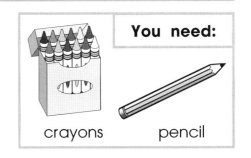

You need:

crayons   pencil

Directions:
Circle each sight word you see. Then color the picture.

Word Bank

he   has

Directions: Practice writing the sight words.

?

Count at the Baseball Field

You need:

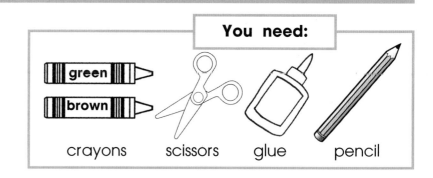

green
brown

crayons   scissors   glue   pencil

Directions:

Color the word "we" green.
Color the word "have" brown.

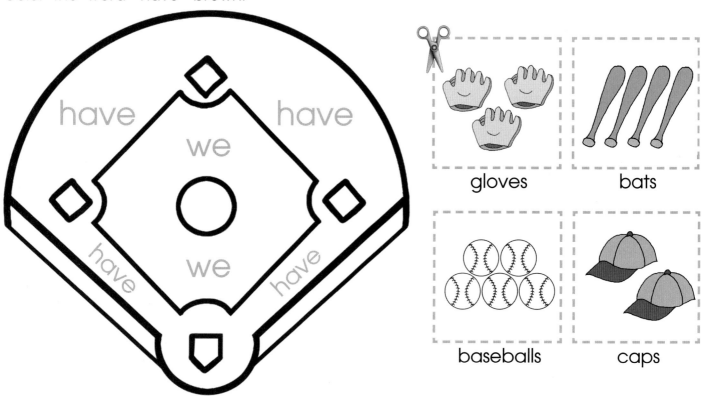

gloves   bats

baseballs   caps

Directions: Practice writing the sight words. Cut and paste pictures to complete the sentences.

we have

3 [   ] .

we have

5 [   ] .

100+ Essential Activities for Sight Words • ©2011 Newmark Learning, LLC

Name _____

Count on Me

Directions:
Connect the circles that show the sight words below.
See the mystery picture.

Word Bank

has   she

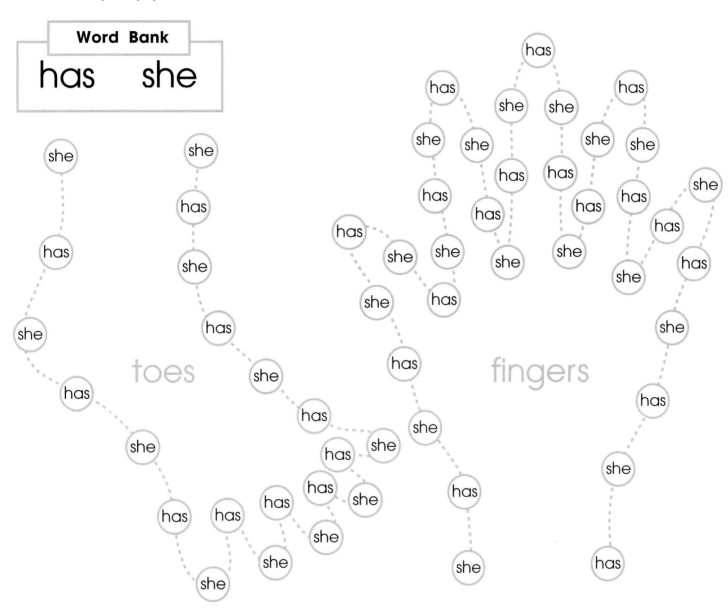

toes

fingers

Directions: Practice writing the sight words.

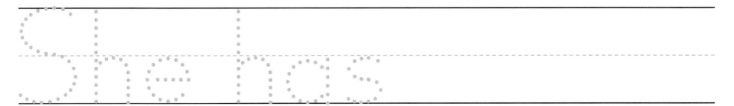

Name _____

Counting With Mom

You need:

crayons   pencil

Directions:
Circle each sight word you see. Then color the picture.

Word Bank			
and	I	mom	see

Directions: Practice writing the sight words.

Mom and I see

Name _____

Finding Shapes With Dad

Directions:

Color each shape according to the key below.

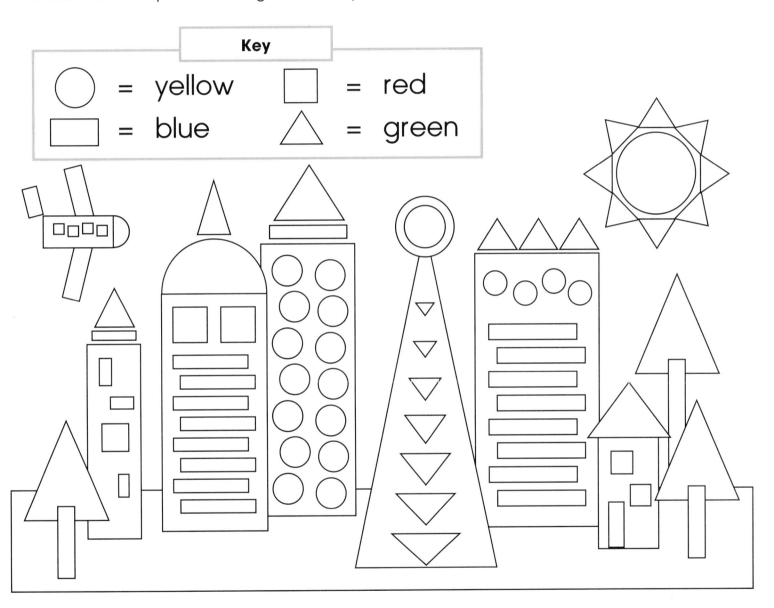

Key			
○ = yellow		□ = red	
▭ = blue		△ = green	

Directions: Practice writing the sight words.

Finding Stripes

Directions:
Cut out the sight words and paste them to complete the sentences.

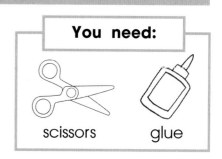
See | the |

chairs
| with |
stripes

| See |
the

umbrellas
with
stripes

See

See | the |

balls
with
stripes

See

| See |
the

sandals
with
stripes

the

---

the

See | the |

sails
with
stripes

the

with

100+ Essential Activities for Sight Words • ©2011 Newmark Learning, LLC

Name _____

Look at the Coins

Directions:
Cut out each word. Then paste the word in the row where it belongs.

Here    .

penny

  is a   .

nickel

Here is a  .

dime

Here is 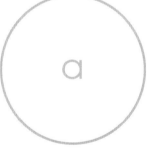 .

quarter

 is a  .

dollar

Name _____

Look at the Shapes

Directions:
Cut out each shape. Then paste the words to complete the sentences.

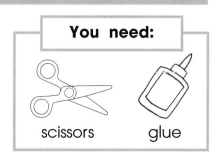

You need:

scissors   glue

 you see the  ?

Can you see the square ?

Can you see the rectangle ?

 you see the 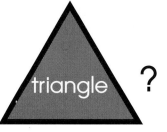 ?

 Can   Can   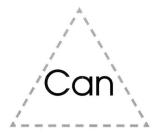 Can    Can

Name _____

On My Desk

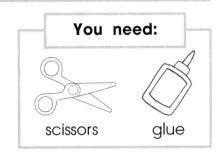

Directions:
Cut and paste the pictures to complete each sentence.

The | pens | are there.

The | erasers | are there.

The | markers | are there.

The | crayons | are there.

The | pencils | are there.

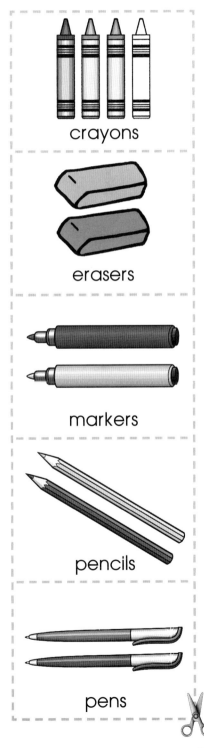

crayons

erasers

markers

pencils

pens

Name _____

Our Tag Sale

Directions:
Cut out each word. Then paste the word in the row where it belongs.

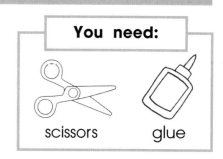
You need:

scissors   glue

We   get a .
dollar

We get  a  .
dime

We  get a  .
nickel

We get  a  .
penny

We get 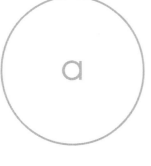 a  .
quarter

 a

 We

 get   a

 get   a

 We

100+ Essential Activities for Sight Words • ©2011 Newmark Learning, LLC

Name _____

Playtime at Home

You need:

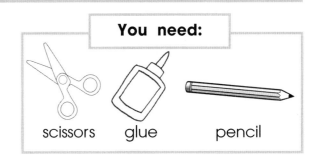

scissors   glue   pencil

Directions:
Practice writing sight words. Cut and paste each picture to complete the sentences.

They play _____ with 1 _basketball_ .

They play _____ with 2 _boats_ .

They play _____ with 3 _planes_ .

They play _____ with 4 _cars_ .

basketball   boats   cars   planes

Name _____

Time to Eat!

Directions:
Practice writing sight words. Cut and paste each picture to complete the sentences.

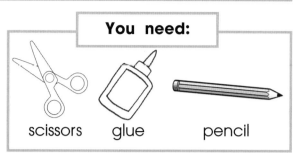
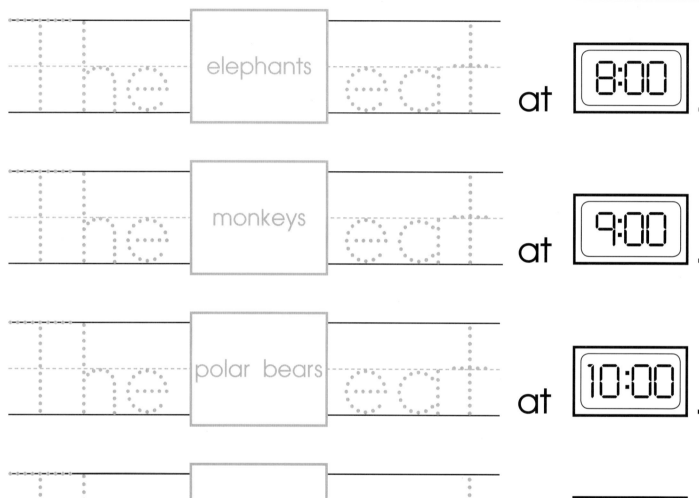

The [elephants] eat at 8:00 .

The [monkeys] eat at 9:00 .

The [polar bears] eat at 10:00 .

The [zebras] eat at 11:00 .

elephants   monkeys   polar bears   zebras

    100+ Essential Activities for Sight Words • ©2011 Newmark Learning, LLC

Name _____

What Has Stripes?

Directions:
Color in the pictures. Cut out the sight words.
Paste them to complete the sentences.

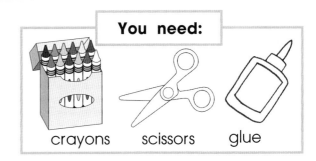
You need:
crayons   scissors   glue

 The       has |||| . stripes

zebra

 The

has

 The   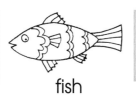   has |||| . stripes

fish

The

has

 The      has |||| . stripes

snake

The

has

 The      has |||| . stripes

tiger

The

has

What Is the Time?

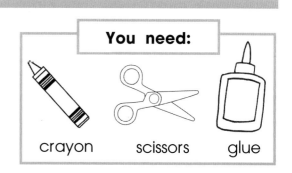
Directions:
Color in the sight words you see below. Practice writing the sight words. Then cut and paste the pictures to complete each sentence.

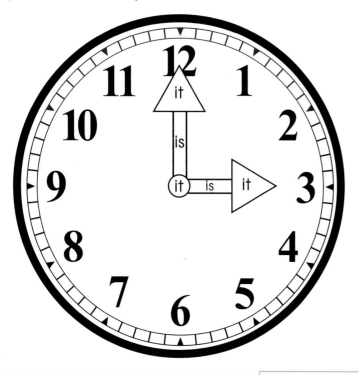

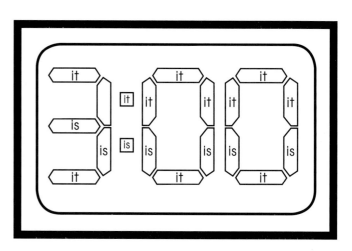

10 o'clock .

2 o'clock .

8 o'clock .

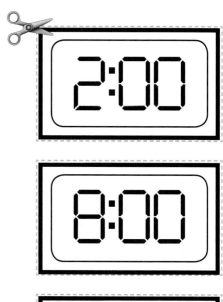

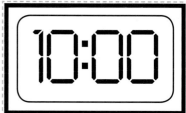

100+ Essential Activities for Sight Words • ©2011 Newmark Learning, LLC

Name _____

At Grandma's House

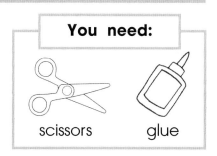
scissors   glue

Directions:
Cut and paste each sight word to complete the sentences.

We	had	cheese .		We
We	had	fruit .		We
We	had	 milk .		We
We	had	 pizza .		We
We	had	popcorn .		We

We

We

We

We

We

had

had

had

had

had

Name _____

At My School

You need:

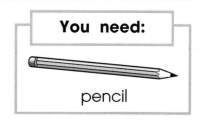

pencil

Directions:
Practice writing sight words.

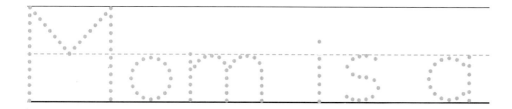

bus driver

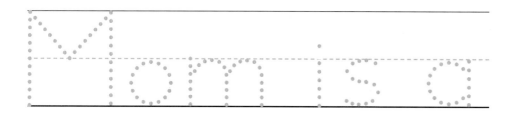

teacher

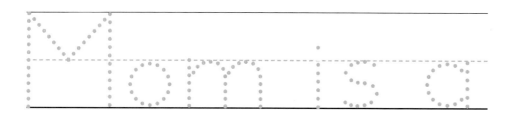

janitor

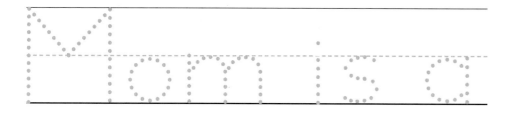

nurse

coach

100+ Essential Activities for Sight Words • ©2011 Newmark Learning, LLC

Name _____

Dad Likes New Clothes

Directions:
Cut and paste each sight word to complete the sentences.

Dad   wants   a   .
vest

Dad   wants   a   .
shirt

Dad   wants   a   .
coat

Dad   wants   a   .
hat

Dad   wants   a   .
sweater

Dad

Dad

Dad

wants

wants

wants

wants

wants

a

a

I Like to Play Sports

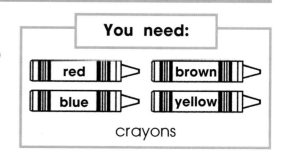

You need:

red   brown
blue   yellow

crayons

Directions:
Color each sight word you see according to the key below.

KEY		
I	=	red
like	=	blue
to	=	brown
play	=	yellow

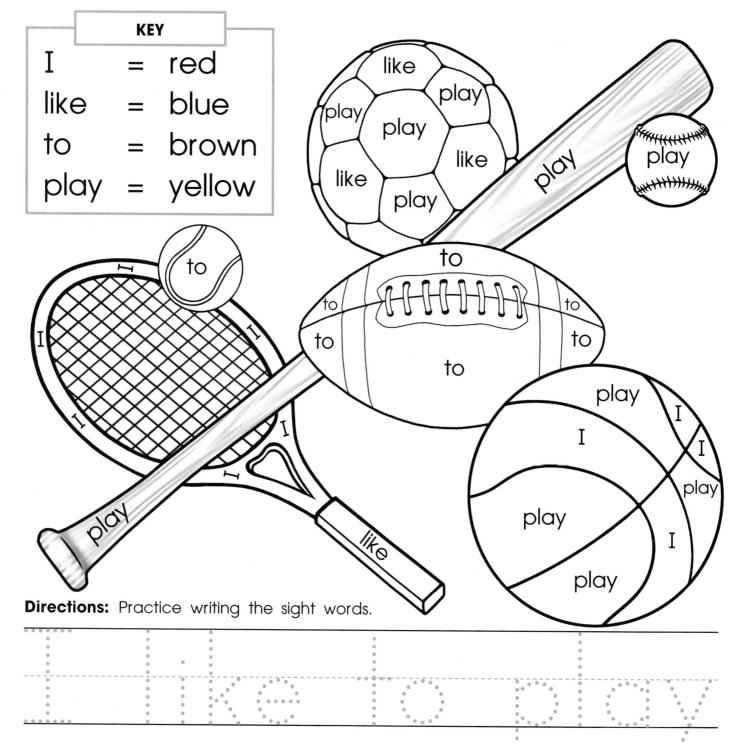

Directions: Practice writing the sight words.

I like to play

100+ Essential Activities for Sight Words • ©2011 Newmark Learning, LLC

Sight Word Readers

Name _____

In Our Town

Directions:
Circle the sight words you see as you go through town.

You need:

pencil

Word Bank

goes   mom   the   to

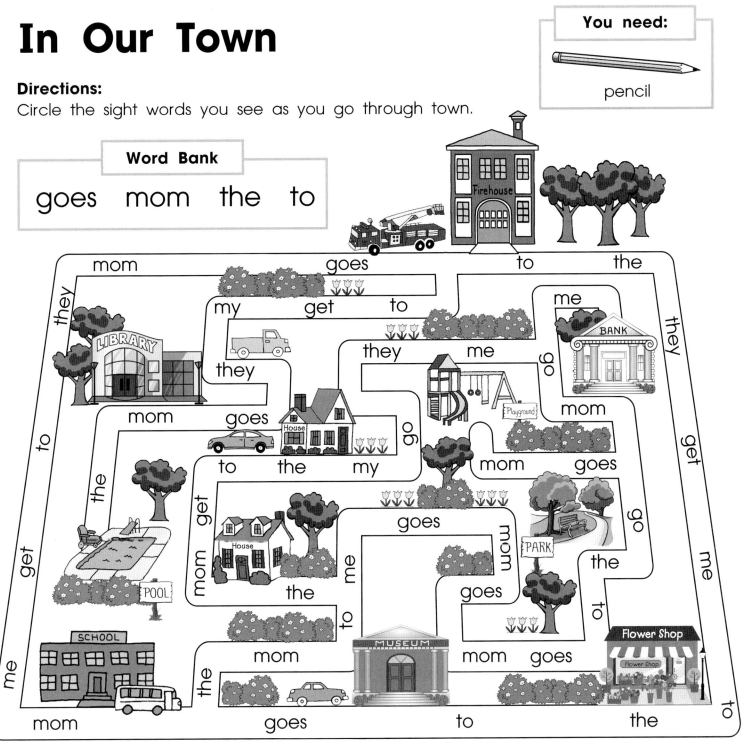

Directions: Practice writing the sight words.

Name _____

In the Band

You need:

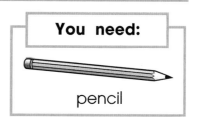

pencil

Directions:
Find the sight words onstage.

Word Bank

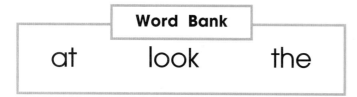

at   look   the

Directions: Practice writing the sight words.

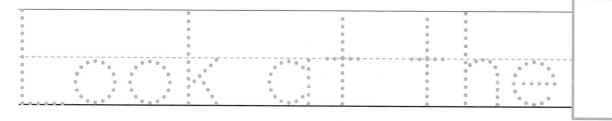

Name _____

Jobs Around Town

Directions:
Cut and paste the sight words to complete each sentence.

We	are	 firefighters .	We
We	are	 police officers .	are
			We
We	are	 doctors .	are
			We
We	are	 teachers .	are
			We
We	are	 chefs .	are

My Family

You need:
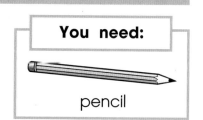
pencil

Directions:
Practice writing sight words. Then draw your family.

Word Bank

is   me   my   this

mom

dad

sister

brother

Name _____

My Favorite Places

Directions:
Follow each sight word to a different place.

Word Bank

I   the   to   went

pool

aquarium

lake

beach

Directions: Practice writing the sight words.

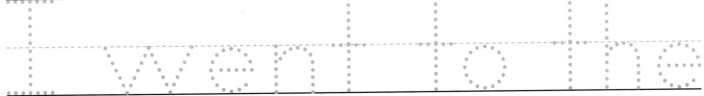

My Home

Directions:
Trace the sight words. Then cut and paste the pictures to complete each sentence.

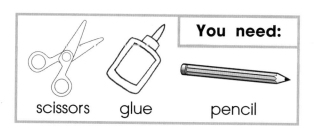

You need:

scissors   glue   pencil

Look at my

Look at my

Look at my

Look at my

house

igloo

houseboat

apartment

Name _____

My Pet

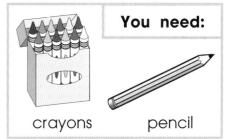

You need:

crayons   pencil

Directions:

Circle each sight word you see. Then color the picture.

Word Bank

likes   me   my

Directions: Practice writing the sight words.

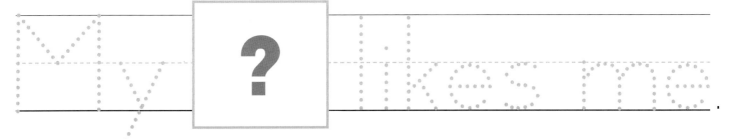

Name _____

My Town

You need:

pencil

Directions:

Circle the sight words you see as you go through town.

Word Bank

here   is   my

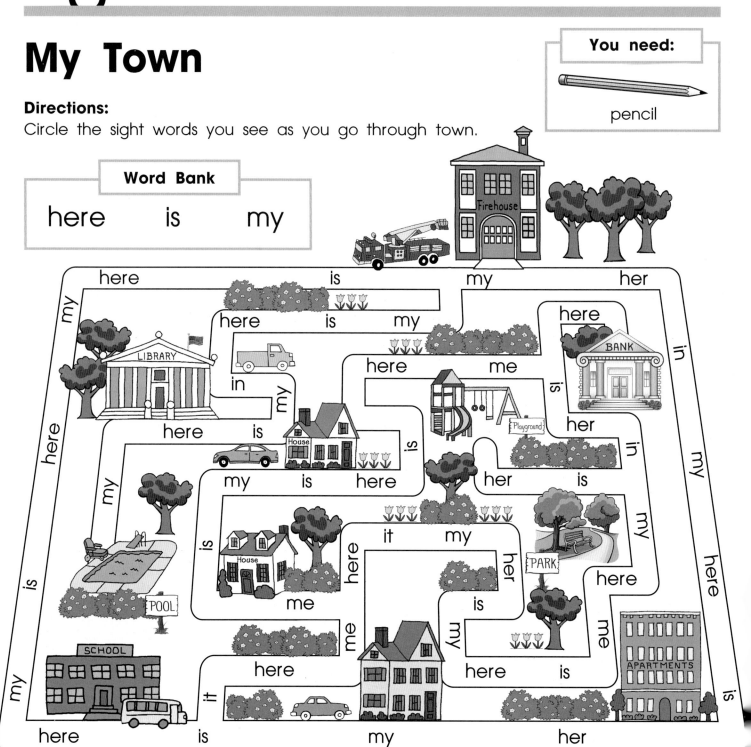

Directions: Practice writing the sight words.

Here is my

?

Name _____

We Go to School

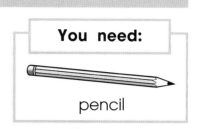
pencil

Directions:
Follow each sight word to a different part of school.

Word Bank

go   the   to   we

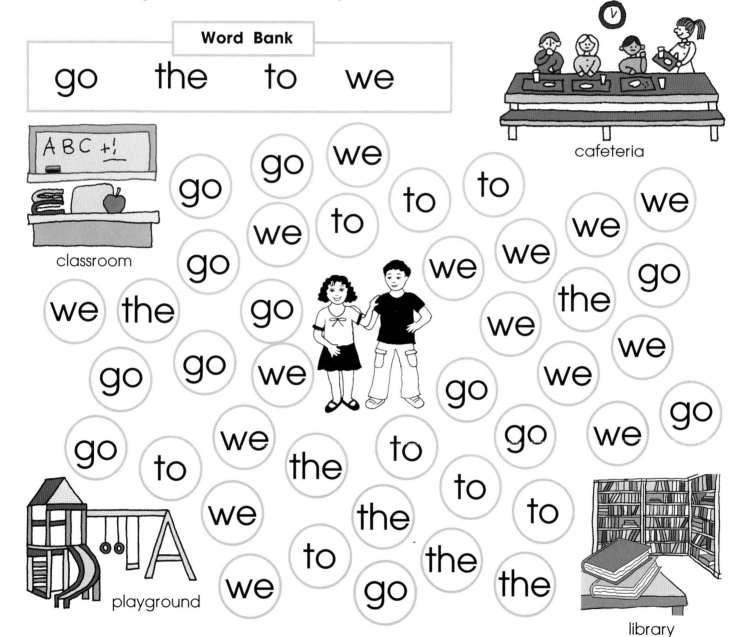

cafeteria

classroom

playground

library

Directions: Practice writing the sight words.

We go to the

?

We Like Birthdays

Directions:
Cut and paste each sight to complete the sentences.

We [like] [the] .
hats

[We] like [the] .
pizza

[We] [like] the .
balloons

We [like] [the] .
piñata

[We] like [the] .
cake

We

We

We

like

like

like

the

the

the

the

When I Grow Up

Directions:
Cut and paste each sight to complete the sentences.

You need:

scissors   glue

I   will   be   a  .
doctor

I   will   be   a  .
farmer

I   will   be   a .
firefighter

I   will   be   a .
pilot

I   will   be   a  .
teacher

will

be

will

be

will

be

will

be

will

be

Name _____

With My Friends

Directions:
Follow each sight word to a different place.

Word Bank

a   all   to   we   went

park

mall

restaurant

cookout

Directions: Practice writing the sight words.

We all went to

Sight Word Memory Game

Directions:

Cut out each word card. Then arrange them upside down in no particular order. Each player turns over two cards per turn. Match up pairs by memorizing the location of each card.

You need:

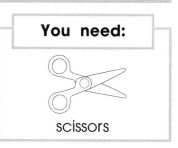

scissors

| a | a | all | all |

Sight Word Memory Game

100+ Essential Activities for Sight Words • ©2011 Newmark Learning, LLC

Sight Word Memory Game

Directions:
Cut out each word card. Then arrange them upside down in no particular order. Each player turns over two cards per turn. Match up pairs by memorizing the location of each card.

You need:

scissors

am	am	and	and
are	are	at	at
be	be	big	big

Sight Word Memory Game

Sight Word Memory Game

Directions:
Cut out each word card. Then arrange them upside down in no particular order. Each player turns over two cards per turn. Match up pairs by memorizing the location of each card.

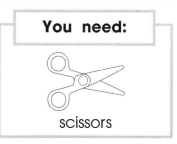
can	can	dad	dad
do	do	down	down
eat	eat	get	get

Sight Word Memory Game

Directions:

Cut out each word card. Then arrange them upside down in no particular order. Each player turns over two cards per turn. Match up pairs by memorizing the location of each card.

You need:

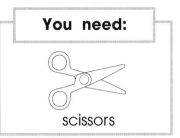

scissors

go	go	goes	goes
had	had	has	has
have	have	he	he

Sight Word Memory Game

Sight Word Readers

Directions:
Cut out each word card. Then arrange them upside down in no particular order. Each player turns over two cards per turn. Match up pairs by memorizing the location of each card.

You need:

scissors

here	here	I	I
in	in	is	is
it	it	like	like

Sight Word Memory Game

100+ Essential Activities for Sight Words • ©2011 Newmark Learning, LLC

Sight Word Memory Game

Directions:
Cut out each word card. Then arrange them upside down in no particular order. Each player turns over two cards per turn. Match up pairs by memorizing the location of each card.

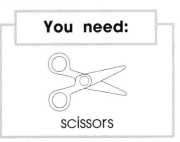
little	little	look	look
me	me	mom	mom
my	my	play	play

Sight Word Memory Game

Directions:
Cut out each word card. Then arrange them upside down in no particular order. Each player turns over two cards per turn. Match up pairs by memorizing the location of each card.

You need:

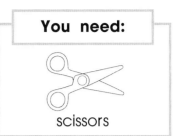

scissors

said	said	see	see
she	she	some	some
that	that	the	the

Sight Word Memory Game

Sight Word Memory Game

Directions:
Cut out each word card. Then arrange them upside down in no particular order. Each player turns over two cards per turn. Match up pairs by memorizing the location of each card.

You need:

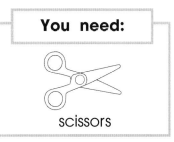

scissors

there	there	they	they
this	this	to	to
up	up	wants	wants

100+ Essential Activities for Sight Words • ©2011 Newmark Learning, LLC

Sight Word Memory Game

Directions:

Cut out each word card. Then arrange them upside down in no particular order. Each player turns over two cards per turn. Match up pairs by memorizing the location of each card.

You need:

scissors

we	we	went	went
will	will	with	with
you	you	🦉	🦉

100+ Essential Activities for Sight Words • ©2011 Newmark Learning, LLC